Be uplifted.
"An Inspired Treasury of Verse"
has been written with
an awareness that our
needs, emotions and sentiments
remain constant
in an ever changing world.

Proud to be Me

I won't wait to be old to be me,
To be blind and regret I can't see;
To be deaf to appreciate sound
Or to lose before I have found;
And the hat that I should throw
away
Will remain on my head anyway.
I will wear whatever I feel.
I shall take, I shall give but not steal.
When I am tired I shall rest,
For that way I'll give of my best;
Won't wait to be told what to do
By friends or family or you
And those who tell me I'm wrong
I'll drown out by singing a song.
I'll eat whatever I need;
Love the flowers but acknowledge
the weed.
I will listen perhaps to advice;
Will smile and appear very nice;
But don't tell me how it should be
For I'm happy just being me!

LYNN NEW ©

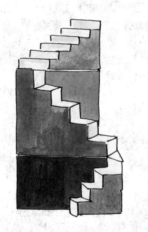

Positive Thinking

There's no such thing as Failure
Except in our own eyes.
We can not always count the stars
Above such cloudy skies.
But they are always up there;
Their light we will attain.
It won't be long before we feel
It's time to start again.
We must not ever feel
One fault will flaw the show,
Or a failure in our wisdom
Will mean we'll never know
How to rectify the past,
Or how to carry on.
Everyone can make mistakes,
We all at times are wrong.
But failure isn't negative
If the positive is sought
And often we learn more, you know,
When experience has taught
That from the bottom step we climb;
Each turning path may show
Not that we have lost our way
But a better route to go.
So do not fret on failure,
You're in good company.
Success is often built you know
On failures memory.

LYNN NEW ©

The Christening Angels

Rest little child
You're christened today
While angels watch over
Your loved ones and pray
That peace will surround you
And health will abound
For angels in glory
Protect and surround.
The font at your blessing,
Your life ever more;
What ever it holds,
What evers in store.
Let sunshine be laughter
And rain showers tears
For both will bring growth
Through childhood years.
Then when you are older
You'll look back and say,
Thank you, dear God
For your angels that day.

LYNN NEW ©

Ode to a Student Nurse
1972

I was once a student nurse
    Many years ago.
I helped to give out medicines
And watched the surgeon sew.
It doesn't bear remembering
    The things we had to do;
Giving out the bed pans,
    Escorting to the 'loo'!
I learnt to give injections
    While lifting up a shirt;
    Thrusting in the needle
While saying, "This won't hurt!"

I can well remember
My long filled student days;
Those stainless steel dishes
    And white enamel trays.
    All the bits and pieces
We had to know by heart;
    All those ward procedures
When filling up a chart.
Folk have a coloured image
Of what a nurse should be:
    A caring gentle angel...
    But was that really me?

LYNN NEW ©

Bringer of Comfort

I shall bring you comfort
Through each earthly plight
And courage through the night time
Till dawn breaks through with light.
I shall show you comfort
In every simple way
And you will feel the warmth of it
As night turns round on day.
I shall bring you comfort,
I shall not let go,
In times of fear of anguish
My spirit you shall know.
Many share my comfort,
All give and all receive
By simply giving of themselves
And learning to believe.

LYNN NEW ©

A Very Special Niece.

You're a niece in a hundred
  So special to me
And when I look closely
  It's then that I see
The warmth of your smile
  The light in your eyes
That lifts all around you
And brightens my skies.
  Though I did not choose
The role you would take
I know I've been blessed
By the difference you make.
  My life's been enriched
By the joy that you give;
  May it be returned
For as long as you live.

LYNN NEW ©

Butterflies and Moths

The butterfly of thought serene
Flutters through each mindful scene,
   Alighting on a memory
   Or resting on a "want to be."
Her gift is pleasure, hopeful dream;
A dancing light through life's sunbeam.

   Yet too the moth, as darkness falls
   Must take to wing as mind recalls
   Each sadness and imagined fear;
      The negative or fallen tear;
   She's silent, dull, no colour bright
   And yet attracted by the light.

   These fragile creatures born of air,
   Within the thinking mind do share
Each hope & dream, each loss & gain;
   Allow them both to wax and wane,
For thought, like wings must dance the sky
   As those of moth and butterfly.

LYNN NEW ©

Shattered Dream

When a treasured dream is shattered
And splinters on the floor
Do not bend and pick it over,
There's danger there, for sure.
Like a mirror that is broken
Each shaft will catch a beam
Of sunlight that may tempt you;
But who will hear you scream,
When it lies in jagged pieces
In the shadows without light
There to tear & catch your footstep
In the darkness of the night?
Don't try now to restore it,
That dream which you once sought,
For mirrors can't be mended,
The image will distort.
If you can not sweep the pieces
From your path on which they lay,
You have to now step round them
And find another way.

LYNN NEW ©

My Garden

Why do I love my garden?
Soon I will tell you why,
But First I want to describe it,
At least in some measure I'll try.

The gate is in need of attention;
The pathway is quite overgrown,
While dandelion dock and clematis
Are the healthiest I've ever known.

The lawn has a striking resemblance
To the pasture on Farmer Joe's land
While the bird bath leans at an angle
With a shallow & deep end unplanned.

The bind weed grows where it shouldn't
While brambles march on through the trees
But the blackbird nests in the lilac
And dragonflies drift on the breeze.

My borders aren't filled to perfection,
My spade spends much time in the shed,
But the bats fly over at evening
And the squirrel comes to be fed.

While birds sing their chorus each morning
And the blue tits fly from their nest
I'll tell you why I love my garden,
It's simply because its been blessed.

LYNN NEW ©

Renewing Your Vows

Love doesn't count the cost
Or make a tally of the debt,
Nor does it hold the hurt
Or pass the blame and yet
At times throughout a marriage true
These things will come to light,
But when the shadows pass away
You'll know it's worth the fight.
So now you stand, resilient both
In love and in shared life
Renewing now your marriage vows
You made as man and wife.
While all the happy times you've shared
Come flooding to the fore
This year your anniversary
Holds very many more.
What better way than now to say
Your promise once again
Through true commitment of your love
Your marriage will remain.
Where once there stood an eager bride
And groom that wedding day,
Now stands a couple greatly loved
And in love will stay.

LYNN NEW ©

The Healthy Option

Cross the road & lick your lips,
You can't resist the smell of chips.
Do not fear the spread on hips,
Make fish your healthy option.

Haddock, plaice, cod large or small,
Scampi, rock, we sell it all.
Come inside or make a call
For fish, the healthy option.

If you want something "on the side"
It doesn't have to be deep fried,
Mushy peas may help decide
On fish, the healthy option.

But if your choice is peas and pies
Or burger buns in choice of size,
We have it all but advertise
Our fish, the healthy option.

Lynn New ©

The Special Race

Take life in your certain stride
Like running in a race,
You'll get there just as easily
If you set your pace.
You may not be the fastest but
Do not be dismayed
The fact you're in the race at all
Shows you've made the grade.
Though some are striking out in front
Not all can take the lead,
Be happy in the running pack
That way you will succeed.
When you've grown you'll realise
The truth of what's been said,
It's better to enjoy the run
Than just be simply led.

LYNN NEW ©

Generation Gap

There were times when I sat with my Grandma
With photographs set on her knee.
Pictures of Mum in the orchard;
My brother with Pop and with me.
Memories spilled from the album,
History turned every page.
I'd sit intrigued and attentive;
A child attracted by age.

The album remained in the family
Long after my grandmother died.
I would often look back on those photos
And the times I sat by her side.
How my grand-daughter calls often to see me
Taking photographs to call her own
Not to add to the album
But to carry around on her phone!

LYNN NEW ©

Your Ninetieth Birthday

Count your birthdays in petals
From sweet smelling Flowers
Not by the candles
Or swift passing hours;
Nor by regret
Of this "coming of age",
Its time now to turn
To an unwritten page.
Measure the years
By the joy you have known,
By Family and Friends
And the love they have shown.
Your life's been Fulfilling
At ninety its true,
Time now to enjoy
Just being you.

LYNN NEW ©

Snippets of...

Help me to know;
When to step forward or to step back,
When to stand still and just be.
When to be hurt and just turn a cheek,
Or cornered and fight to be free.
When to show love, peace and
                                compassion,
When to hold tight or let go.
How to live life setting example,
How to be me... how to grow.

... Thought

LYNN NEW ©

What did yesterday teach?
What will I learn tomorrow?
Only the fact that I live today
   Richer for joy and sorrow.
Brighter for lessons subtly taught,
Wise through experience gained.
Nothing is wasted, forgotten or lost
When the spirit of peace is attained.

Diamond Anniversary

On your diamond anniversary
You both have reached the stage
Where you value every blessing
Though complain perhaps of age.
Now your memories are golden
Through your hair runs silver thread
Yet your love as strong as diamonds
Has sparkled since you wed.
For sixty years you've chosen
To live as man and wife
And so today we celebrate
Your loving married life.

LYNN NEW ©

The Older Man

Feeling deflated, over the hill?
Reach for the bottle, reach for the pill.
Can't climb the stairs without feeling a twinge
Or reaching Monday without the odd winge?
Like to look forward, but often look back;
Sleep in the chair instead of the sack?
Not losing your hair, what can I say?
For all that there is, it's sure turning grey.
Not only a dad, but grandfather too,
Who would have thought it, for someone like you?
Like to pull birds ~ perhaps in your dreams,
You value true friendship & all that it means.
Don't be discouraged, your age I can't tell,
It's more than enough to know you are well
More than enough for you're doing just fine
And its more than enough...
To know you are mine.

LYNN NEW ©

Passage of Time

Nothing of the past will change,
It's over, done.
The Future's rather different,
It's what's to come.
The past now can not hurt you
It's memory.
The Future's more uncertain
It's what's to be.
The past can be remembered
With ribbon tied,
But the Future flies on wings;
Dreams undenied.
The past can be forgotten,
Put out of sight,
But the Future's early dawning
Must see the light.
The past is very rigid,
It will not bend,
But the Future holds the healing
Of what must mend.
So think about the past
But do not dwell;
Of the Future that may scare you
Only time will tell.
Of one thing do be certain,
We all walk on,
Turning Future into present;
That's where we belong.

LYNN NEW ©

PAST

PRESENT FUTURE

Your Eighteenth Birthday

Eighteen is a magic age
When you can stand on centre stage
And do most things you've wanted to
While to yourself alone be true.

A certain Freedom is now gained
Responsibility attained.
A mile stone to celebrate
A birthday that will be just great.

Stand tall, be proud, we'll raise a cheer
For it's not just another year
But one that you must surely see
As reaching your maturity.

LYNN NEW ©

The Fullest Moon

Dark was the night,
Like velvet shroud
That kissed the moon
With skirted cloud.
Veiled in her fullness
Her celebrated form.
Shadowed in her brilliance
By each passing storm.
Yet she rode the heavens
Drenching them with light,
Her silver gown of moonshine
Dancing in the night.
She sparkled in the puddles,
Spangled on the sea,
While the magic of that moonshine
Fell silently on me.
As if in celebration
My spirit danced its tune
That echoed down from heaven
And the fullness of the moon.

LYNN NEW ©

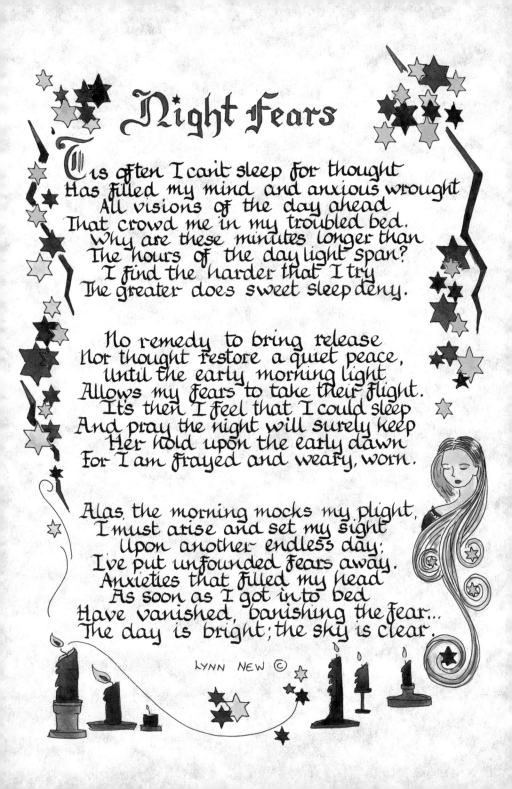

Night Fears

'Tis often I can't sleep for thought
Has filled my mind and anxious wrought
All visions of the day ahead
That crowd me in my troubled bed.
Why are these minutes longer than
The hours of the day light span?
I find the harder that I try
The greater does sweet sleep deny.

No remedy to bring release
Nor thought restore a quiet peace,
Until the early morning light
Allows my fears to take their flight.
It's then I feel that I could sleep
And pray the night will surely keep
Her hold upon the early dawn
For I am frayed and weary, worn.

Alas, the morning mocks my plight,
I must arise and set my sight
Upon another endless day;
I've put unfounded fears away.
Anxieties that filled my head
As soon as I got into bed
Have vanished, banishing the fear...
The day is bright; the sky is clear.

LYNN NEW ©

Dream Boat

Let go forward
Let go aft,
It is not a bed you're in
But a sailing craft.
Pull up fenders,
Bow waves washing white.
You'll be sleepy sailing
Silently through night.
Leave your day time jetty,
Heading out to sea;
Body quietly resting
Mind and spirit free.
Let your dream boat take you
All around the world,
Cutting through life's ocean
With your sails unfurled.
Sailing for adventure,
Riding out a wave,
Perhaps to talk to monsters,
My! you're very brave.
Nothing you can't handle,
Nothing you can't do;
Enjoying every moment...
Too soon your journey's through.
Night time stars are fading,
The harbour master calls,
Return now to the jetty
Before the tide falls.
Make fast forward
Soon to come ashore...
You're lying in your bed again
~A sailing boat no more.

LYNN NEW ©

Thirtieth Birthday

When you reach eighteen
Or forty, or more,
Or given the key
To the twenty-first door,
You'd celebrate well
Each milestone met,
But at thirty your birthday
Must be the best yet.
You've reached a high peak
But not "over the hill",
There are mountains to climb
Out there for you still.
You're learning through life
That experience shows
The older the more
Your confidence grows.
But let no one tell you
You have to let go
Of youth for in age
You must gracefully grow.
Enjoy being thirty
And the world you live in
For the rest of your life
Is about to begin.

LYNN NEW ©

Nephew Defined

Nephew, what's a nephew?
  It's easy to define,
  Totally unique and yet
In some way one of mine.
  A turn of head, a cheery smile,
  The clues are there to see,
You're one of us, no doubt at all,
  My nephew definitely.
Yet I would choose you as a friend
  To trust, respect and share
The special moments in my life,
  Knowing that you care.
For blood may be the bonding
  And family the tie,
You mean far more than that to me
  So listen while I try
To tell you that you're worthy
  And tell you that I'm proud
And that by choice, at any time
  I'd choose you from the crowd.

LYNN NEW ©

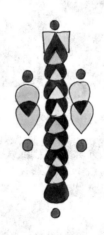

Balancing Life

It is good to be,

Loving but not dutiful
Responsive but not manipulated,
Needing but never needy,
Independent but not solitary.

Aware of yourself without being selfish;
Angry, without being hurtful,
Be in the wrong and ask for forgiveness
Or in the right without feeling superior.

Helpful but not condescending
Emotional but not melodramatic;
Giving without becoming a martyr.
A pupil but also a teacher.

It is good to be aware of what life
can teach you.

LYNN NEW ©

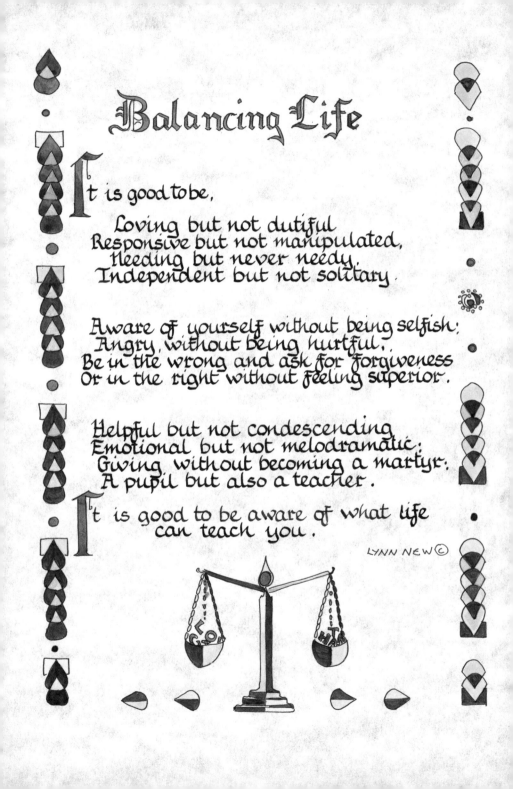

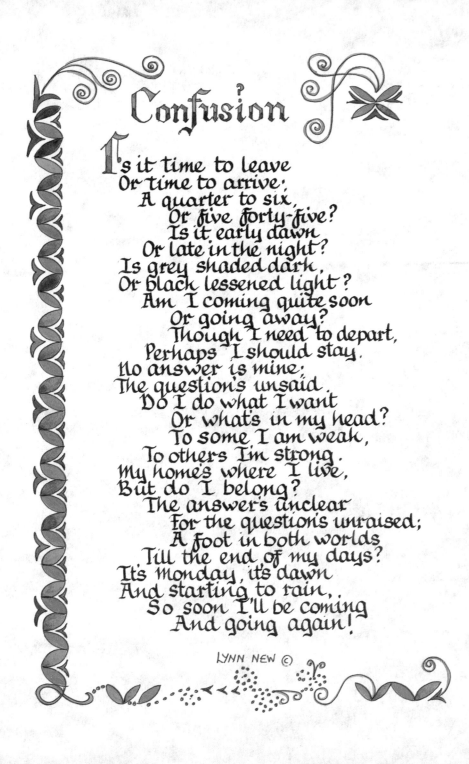

Confusion

Is it time to leave
Or time to arrive;
A quarter to six,
     Or five forty-five?
     Is it early dawn
Or late in the night?
Is grey shaded dark,
Or black lessened light?
     Am I coming quite soon
          Or going away?
          Though I need to depart,
     Perhaps I should stay.
No answer is mine;
The question's unsaid.
     Do I do what I want
          Or what's in my head?
          To some I am weak,
     To others I'm strong.
My home's where I live,
But do I belong?
     The answer's unclear
          For the question's unraised;
          A foot in both worlds
     Till the end of my days?
It's Monday, it's dawn
And starting to rain,
     So soon I'll be coming
          And going again!

Consulting Your Doctor

Can you offer medication
  Or a sympathetic word,
A smile of consolation
On a problem simply heard?
Can you offer understanding,
  Or wisdom to the wise,
While sincere appreciation
  Is mirrored in your eyes?

If you answer all these questions
  And do not have to guess;
Though some may be in negative,
  Some positively 'yes'.
Then sit for consultation,
  My time is yours to fill
And I promise as your G.P.
  I won't tell you why I'm ill!

I will hide my indigestion,
Won't hold my aching head,
Won't talk of constipation,
But prescribe for you instead.
But when you stand on leaving
Could you spare a thought and say,
  "You ought to see a doctor
  For you don't look well today!"

LYNN NEW ©

Better Still

Flowers would be nice;
A card would do the trick
    To help to cheer you up
If you are feeling sick.

A letter through the door;
    A message on the phone
Would help you now to know
    That you are not alone.

    A basket would be fine
Of fruit to make your day.
    Apples are the thing
    To keep the 'doc' away.

I can not quite decide
    What is best to do;
    I'm sorry that you're ill
For I think the world of you.

    I'd like to cheer you up
In all these ways and more
    Encouraging good health...
For that's what friends are for!

LYNN NEW ©

Falling Leaves

Why falls the leaf that spirals down
From trees immortal gloried crown
And drops through Autumns breezeless day,
Till on the ground in death does lay.
Its brothers join it as a crowd,
Till earth full wears them as a shroud,
Covered as a blanket should:
The trees now bare within the wood.

When golden leaves in death are thrown
'Tis nature caring for her own,
Protecting beast and plant and flower
From winters blast and darkest hour.
If only man a leaf would take
From natures book, his own to make
And suffer not the winter long
But in his breast hear springtimes song.

LYNN NEW ©

Heaven Sent

You didn't know me well,
    Yet loved me true
For you were part of me
    And I of you.
I had to touch this earth,
    Our hearts entwine,
For truly I was yours
    And you were mine.
By coming so to you
    You took the role
Allowing me to live
And then in Christ made whole.
You made your sacrifice
    In letting go
And only those who share
    Will ever know.
I knew I could not stay
    Yet had to be
With you for a while
    And you with me.
Dear Mum, may peace be yours;
    I came to you through choice
And now I grow in Light.
    As one, let us rejoice.

LYNN NEW ©

A Quiet Place

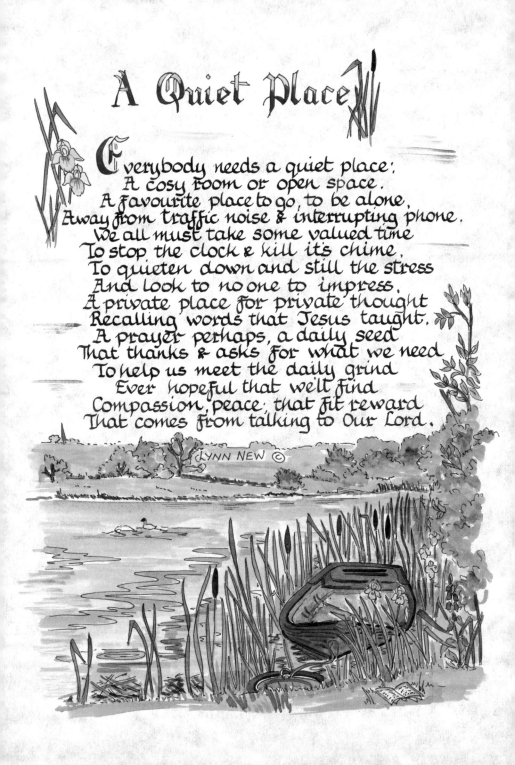

Everybody needs a quiet place;
A cosy room or open space.
A favourite place to go, to be alone,
Away from traffic noise & interrupting phone.
We all must take some valued time
To stop the clock & kill it's chime,
To quieten down and still the stress
And look to no one to impress.
A private place for private thought
Recalling words that Jesus taught.
A prayer perhaps, a daily seed
That thanks & asks for what we need
To help us meet the daily grind
Ever hopeful that we'll find
Compassion, peace; that fit reward
That comes from talking to Our Lord.

LYNN NEW ©

Dear Daughter-in-Law

You're more like a daughter
Than daughter in law,
We value your friendship
And so much more,
For we gained a daughter
It has to be said
And our hearts rejoiced
The day you both wed.

We couldn't have chosen
Someone like you
To marry our son
And if you only knew
You have enriched
Each life and each heart.
In all that we feel
You play a huge part.

Perhaps not our daughter
But you have become
Loved and respected
By this Dad and Mum.
So if you have need
Or something to share
Please do remember
We'll always be there.

LYNN NEW ©

Natures Way

Let me walk your rutted paths
 Let me make my way
'Cross the meadow, to the stile,
 Let me breathe, I pray
The scent of bells, dressed in blue,
 Of blossom from the tree;
The smell of earth and early dew
 And wood anemone.

Fill my ears with calling birds,
 Fill my eyes with light
Dappled down from shaded trees;
 A startled wren takes flight,
Silent feather falls to ground
 To rest on mossy bank,
While creatures stir and thrive unseen
 In leaf mould, cool and dank.

Let my life be thine oh Lord
 And yet in wisdom see
The beating pulse within Your world
 That whispers to me... FREE!

LYNN NEW ©

Watchful Fairy

I shall Fly on gossamer wings
Through mists of dream filled sleep,
Till on your shoulder gently rest
My vigil there to keep.
A sudden breeze or movement;
A noise or whisper heard
Shall tell you that I'm with you
Though you'll not hear a word.
I'll not be there to hinder
Or weave a magic spell,
Just to show I love you
And that I wish you well.
I'll be there in the morning
As you switch on the light
And stay with you at length until
You go to sleep at night.

LYNN NEW